THE BORDER SURROUNDS US

BY KAREN CONNELLY

The Small Words in My Body (1990)

Touch the Dragon: A Thai Journal (1992, non-fiction)

This Brighter Prison: A Book of Journeys (1993)

One Room in a Castle: Letters from Spain,
France & Greece (1995, non-fiction)

The Disorder of Love (1997)

The Border Surrounds Us (2000)

THE BORDER
SURROUNDS US

KAREN CONNELLY

M&S

Canadian Cataloguing in Publication Data

Connelly, Karen, 1969-
The border surrounds us

Poems.
ISBN 0-7710-2245-X

PS8555.O546B67 2000   C811'.54   C00-930328-6
PR9199.3.C66B67 2000

We acknowledge the financial support of the Government of Canada through the Book Publishing Industry Development Program for our publishing activities. We further acknowledge the support of the Canada Council for the Arts and the Ontario Arts Council for our publishing program.

Typeset in Adobe Garamond by M&S, Toronto
Printed and bound in Canada

McClelland & Stewart Inc.
The Canadian Publishers
481 University Avenue
Toronto, Ontario
M5G 2E9

1 2 3 4 5   04 03 02 01 00

For the people of the border

. . . the truth, as I see it at least, is that the artist is groping his way in the dark just like the man in the street — incapable of separating himself from the world's misfortune and passionately longing for solitude and silence; dreaming of justice, yet being himself a source of injustice; dragged — even though he thinks he is driving it — behind a chariot that is bigger than he . . .

— Albert Camus
from *Resistance, Rebellion, and Death:*
The Artist and His Time

CONTENTS

PART FOUR

I

The Vacation

I.

The blue churn of the sea
fused her green heart.
She was born to the tribe
of terrible longings,
lungs to gills,
skin to scales.

When the breakers choked her,
she swam farther,
and the fishermen
on the shore stared in horror.
One remarked to the other:

crazy stupid
fuckin white girl.

Later, his slender brown hands examining
her coral-torn knees,
Daniel whispered,
They thought you were
drowning yourself.

The enormity
of his eyes frightened her.
He was asking
if it was true.

2.

Wild-eyed but calm,
salted, filleted,
ready to be eaten,
she watched the men hoisting
crates of shark and lobster,
the most beautiful
black, glistening
the only gods
she had ever seen,
their thighs as big
as her waist, tendoned with
the muscle of the sun.

And the women –
to be so alive –
the women dazzled.
She had learned in art class
black is the absence
of colour, but the women
were rainbows and her eyes
could not find the end of them.

In the cane fields
the people came out to meet her,
the people walked out
of the cane onto the road
speaking a language like honey
in sea-water, green water,
cane juice, their voices
held secrets, the fine dust
was alive on their feet.

A woman laid an ivory-palmed
black hand
on her cheek
and the girl kissed that hand.

Later, walking back
through the white
rich walled neighbourhoods,
the jagged glass,
the nail heads embedded
in the concrete edges,
she knew she had returned
to the killing labyrinth,
so many white walls.

3.

The bougainvillea blazed scarlet
and orange over the broken glass
and nails, out of reach.

But she leaned over
and touched Daniel,
stroked through him
so lightly, as though
skin were water, as though
it were possible to be
clean always, to kiss
the sweetwater mouth

without the landlady
barging in, hissing
filthy
that stupid bitch
screaming he had to leave.

Whatever wants in
will get in
somehow.
She made a vow
to fling open
every door and
every window
in her life.

An enormous centipede
slithered in from the garden.
Swallows dove over the fruit
on the kitchen table, catching
the last humming flies of dusk.
While she slept
naked under a sheet,
a thief came in, too.

He stole her gold and silver
and copper bracelet
but left her
untouched,
anxious
to be taken.

The Story

Eventually each of us
will tell a story
of scars and ocean,
the way you never
know what's in deeper water
while the seaweed shadows
twist below you
and the slow fear
fills your thin arms.

You know you are a fool
for having come this far.
You know you could never
swim fast enough.
In your mouth your heart
dissolves like a holy tablet
of salt.

In the end, it is
only a drifting body
of wood. Or a dolphin.

But what we own
beyond a shadow
of a doubt
is our fear
of being eaten
alive, torn apart
in depths we have entered
willingly.

The Dancer

Desire ruptures
the dumb sleep
of the world.

For this reason
we do not rest
in our cages
but bite the metal bars
and gnaw our wrist bones,
follow the prophet on our knuckles
and slide our fingers
too slowly
through the flame.

Desire, rising:
this is why we claw our way
through each other's bodies,
through the innocent earth.

In our becoming
we are broken,
as the first cell splits
into life. The shedding snake
knows it, and the sapling
cracked by spring ice,
and the river rushing away
from its pure source

and the dancer
planing down the bones
of his feet.

We are taken apart even
as we crouch down
among the stones
unable to fit
the many fragments
together, unable to find
the lost key to ourselves.

The lucky among us learn
to break the rusted locks.
The locksmith demands,
    Why can't you just be still
    with these locks on your hands,
    your mouth?
    They are fine mechanisms,
    they allow you to speak
    and to eat and
    to clap like a seal.

    Why can't you be still?

The dancer hurls his body
into time
time runs down
his spine
like a child
dragging a stick
along an iron fence.

Those of us
who never argue
with gravity
witness the length of him
strike the floor
and soar upward,
animal like us
but angel also

cradle for the mad heart,
    ribs gleam through
        the curved back

vertebrae shine and roll
    like enormous pearls

his legs strike wild
        two pale horses swimming
        in sunstruck water

But the dancer knows.
His own heart burns down
its blackened wick.
He feels it first
in his feet:
time reaching the end
of its long iron fence.

The Blessing Scars

Far beneath that smooth smile,
the scars begin.
They seem endless.
But your face, with its
tooth-glint and arched brow,
gives no wound away.
You have charmed the devil
with just a cigarette
and a blow job.
You have lifted souvenirs
from death's stainless steel shop.

The long splits in your
chest and belly are
like skull fissures,
the extended brain of the body
still dreaming underneath.
Or they are the marks of a man
who shark-danced
and burst with a white face
out of the red sea.

The surgeon lifted out your stomach,
slung your lungs over
your sheeted shoulders, dangled
the gleaming pumps and dripping engines
down your ribcage.
They pulled everything out of you
to find the filigree chain of your spine
and probe each link of your life.

Which one was weak?
Which one was strong enough?
The heart thumping on the table
was frightened by the cold.

Your spirit swam up, deeper and deeper
into the sterilized air.
Your spirit floated under the lamps,
swam as you used to swim, a child
in the pool at night,
the wavering light elongating
your limbs blue and frog-like.

The spirit stared down at its body,
your own frog-gutted, white-bellied body,
and your spirit was baffled
by its choice:
the infinite green ladders of air
or flesh with fresh wounds.

How would any spirit choose?

Oh, friend, you were lucky
beyond ordinary luck. The blessing
was more than a white-god word.

On the far shore, a great wind
tore singing through the yew tree.
The capillaries of wood
trembled, unclenched –
tiny fingerbones begged the sky

and you woke sewn-up alive.

The Cowgirl

for Mara

It is not hard for me
to imagine you,
the quiet one
who has mastered bluntness
and bluster, the loud raw
jokes of cowhands.
You are the other sister.
The one who lives.

The field is snow flayed by wind,
welts of raw earth showing through
like the welts on the horse's flanks.
Or perhaps not.
Perhaps the mare's scars
are in her mind, and harder to heal.
Maybe there is no snow yet.
Perhaps her terror is pure memory,
the last human touch,
the beating to the head,
across the eyes, the blow
that tore her away
from the two-legged voices
of the earth.

You are there in the frozen field
with the stamping mare.
She is twenty feet away.

You stand still, looking into her,
searching for her
the way some women search
for religion or love.
Yes: the way you talk to her
is like a prayer.
You ask for her to *Come come,*
meaning out of hell.
You say, *Easy, girl, easy,*
knowing nothing
painful ever is.

She stands there, one eye rolled
half-white as the blown snow,
the black forelock twisted
round the taut brown ear.
Hot breath comes like smoke
out of your nostrils and hers.

Now the bay mare turns
her head this way, that way,
as though walking through
dense brush.
You will her to remember
the scent of trust
on a hand.

Eyes watering now, you wonder
about brutality and love,
the human who shot
fear into the mare's brain
and the human who stands
there on numb feet.

How long can you wait
for what you cannot save?

Eyelashes thick with frost,
you finally turn away,
biting white skin
from your lips.

You are a woman
walking home
across the fields

with a horse

far behind

following.

The Moment

Back of the orchards
opens the deep ravine,
the wildness at the edge of order.
Bears down there, they say, and coyotes
barking below the bone-pale cliffs.
Crumbling hoodoo faces stare
into the dark ruckus of trees.

For a while I searched
for a path into that adventure,
then gave up, seduced instead
by winter apples.

Mid-December, the trees are without leaves
but a few yellow apples cling
and glow like sunlit gems.
They are better than the apples
of high-season leaf and green.
They are the rare, uneaten apples
of the world. They did not fall
and fill the shallows of the field
like red and ochre pebbles in the silt-beds
of certain rivers. They are not
the apples picked and tumbled
into the great wooden crates.
They are not bought
and sold apples, these,
but gift apples.

The chill flesh and juice
sting my teeth.
The globe turns in my fingers
until I have swallowed it whole.

The entire field smells
of cold apples. And, at the edge
of the ravine, pungent sage finds
its way into my apple-filled
pockets, my mouth.
Sage, Russian thistle, sere grass.
The land keeps her heart
close to desert while her body
rolls down luxuriant
to the raw-silver lake.

At the place where
the orchard stumbles and falls
into the ravine,
a deer appears.
First as noise among the brush,
and now as a white nose floating
through the poplar branches.

Then up, openly,
into the naked orchard,
a young mule buck.
There are no apples left down there.
He eats the dry scraps of autumn.

When the wind turns
he pauses, lifting his head into the air
of my scent. He poises himself
near the ledge of his body,
ready to bolt.
His eyes scout back
and forth along the cliffs,
trying to see the smell of me.

I crouch in the sage,
gazing down,
holding my breath,
knowing it cannot last:
soon he will strike
the drum in the ground
with his hoof and
bound down the ravine
like the stag in an old painting,
unhuntable, unholdable,
leaping forever
into the great trees.

For a moment we stare directly
into the black gleam
of each other's eyes.

Then he is gone.

II

The Darkness Above Mandalay

In the darkness above Mandalay
she is wondering how
to carry them:
the suitcases, the letters
for the exiles, the dirty
blades of history.

Down below, men with scars
on their ankles
are dreaming.
Down below, the people
eat silence
while their hearts
fill with thunder.

One life
and the wide earth
bound, lodged in her gut
like a nugget of new jade,
like a bullet.

She wants to say *love*
but the word is spoiled.
She wants to say *fierce*
but it fails.
Half a dozen languages but not
a word for what she knows now.

Maybe the beggars in Tachilek.
Maybe the bloated dog
in the river that divides two nations.
What she means is the children
playing there
after the body floated by.

Remember how they stared up at her,
broke her with their eyes,
put her back together
with their voices:
filthy children
in the river, laughing,
getting clean
despite everything.

Prison Entrance

In Chiang Rai she listened to the men
in prison listening to the radio.
For hours, the King's jazz and sparrows,
news about skirmishes on the border.

Sometimes their voices, their shouts,
were so clear. So clear she wondered
about the secrets behind
the high grey walls, the worlds
she could not fathom, with freedom
wrapped around her like a cape
she could never pull off.

A playground beside the wall, an art gallery.
No surprise in this, nothing but the truth
of contradiction. In every convict,
a child's face, somewhere
a window not made of metal,
fingerprints a rainbow
painting on paper.

The sun pinkened, dripped down
the sky, not red at all but the colour
of nuclear watermelon, oval and glowing.

Mosquitoes borrowed blood from her
bare ankles, her hands.
The unseen men moved on the other side,
hidden from the trees and silent houses.
The sky melted down very quickly.

When the narrow path
darted into the night
like a grey lizard,
she rose, she went forward.
She could not resist it.

She walked
through the wall.

The Mon Fishermen

We thought they were mermaids,
the women in the heart of the bay,
rising black out of the water,
silhouettes lifting nets of fish
into the sky.

There where the hills sweep down
in a green deluge to the sea,
and Horse Island rears out
of the blue like a mount breaking
from heaven, not water.

Everything turns over, everything
is a clue for some other mystery
but never the mystery of itself.
We wake and wash from our faces
the essence of not-knowing.

In seconds, the wind changes
the tide draws out, crashes in,
the coastline gives way
to another kingdom.

Suddenly the women in the heart
of the bay are fishermen
with nets, not hair, draped
around their necks.

Suddenly they are close to you,
so close you feel their eyes
coming in like boats
to haunt your face.

They rise before you,
arms weighted with silver,
a treasure of fish,
their human flesh
made of salt water, scars, sky.
Their mouths burn white
beneath their sea-black eyes.

The Portrait

for Daw Aung San Suu Kyi

Cut through the canvas, my face.
See the country writhing behind me.

Barbed wire garlands the old house
like a giant's crown.

The woman behind the gate
wears yellow flowers in her hair.

Twisted round her throat
and ankles and wrists

are the ropes of voices, the braided
red commandments of the dead.

At night alone in the old house
she understands everything

was inevitable, step after step
into the dumb mouths of the guns

into the room of slit-eye and boot
then beyond, into the future's country.

You will see her, years later, in portrait:
a small exhausted woman sitting upright

(she never lets her back
touch the back of her chair)

her beauty grown keen as her bones,
whetted, the tongue of a knife.

She holds the blade in her hand, hilt forward.
Yes: she is offering you a weapon.

Fine Jade Bracelet

In northern Burma, the Kachin men who work government-operated jade mines are often paid for their labour in heroin instead of money.

Jade pits.
The green eyes of the earth gouged out.
The miners crawl up like insects
dying in the glow of dusk.
In the heart of the mines
the only sound among rasping picks
and human lungs
is the massive creak
of shifting stone.
When the stone falls
the camp women wail
down the valley
like mythical creatures,
but they are only women
screaming.

The needle is silent going down
into the brown skin, the red salt veins.
The general who owns the mountain said
   The bodies of the people are quarries.
Green bracelets glimmer
on the strong wrists
of China and America.

In the street of small sparrows,
past the noodle stands and the hiss
of hot oil, the tea shops
fill with Kachin men, brothers
through blood and sorrow.
The needles pass between them
like gestures of futile love,
like cigarettes.

One of them bows his head
and places the rope of jasmine
in your hand
without touching you.
The royal gesture, the gesture
of servility, his elbow
held with the opposite hand:
jasmine the only jewel
you can keep here.

He sings in the narrow lane,
half-naked under the light.
He pours water over his head,
drowning the blue tiger
tattooed on his back.

The Stormful Gardener

The symbol of political resistance in Burma
is the fighting peacock.

I.

The peacock is gone
from your garden, banished
by the neighbours, who could not
tolerate the screams at dusk,
that song torn from red silk and salt.

The peacock is fled, its turquoise eyes
cast down the night, blind.
Now that iridescence shimmers
green, shines blue in the lanes
of your memory.

Streets of whitewashed brick open there,
with boys running through tea shops.
The aluminum kettles familiar
as faces. And, oh, book stalls.
Even now, the Buddha's gold hand
bears a common brown sparrow.
Shadows play on a wall
you have not seen
for ten years,
a child's whole life.
Or the length of your
brother's prison sentence.

Now the generals devour
the holy bones and jewels,
children's fingers, the tongues
and hearts of your people.

There is no way out of this.
A poem is not an escape path,
nor a jungle to hide in.
No explanation explains
and the poet presumes nothing
but a common knowledge:
for the greater sorrow,
there is no balm.

You turn your shoulder
against history and push.
One shoulder buckles and
you shift your weight
to the other.

Shoring up each word,
you heave your mind against an army.
With tenacity, you work, night-eyed.
Lithe and quick, you work,
without letting go.
A mongoose spirit.

2.

You build a garden.

You belong to that particular breed:
the stormful gardener.
The restless one, the man
who is never still
in his green kingdom.

Always a tendril to be clipped,
a papery blossom to pluck here,
there a patch of dry soil.
Your hands smell of the earth.
The ivory cockatoo walks away
through the flame trees
and must be captured
with a solemn tenderness.
The doves need feeding.

Every garden requests
a very long dance.
Thus you move among the roses
and purple faces
of orchids, you peer
into the soil and pivot
the red clay pots to
a new slant of sun.
Butterflies pause
to taste each brilliance.

Shadows fall and land
on your face like blue petals.
The cockatiel grows jealous
of the grander cockatoo
and you must attend
to this imbalance
of affection.
Fuchsia bougainvillea
ignites the fences.

You breathe the air at midnight.
You consult the rainbows around the moon
and consider the rain's strength
against your open hand.

I wonder about your dreams.

Whether you dream wars
or waterfalls spilling
from your fingers,
your own body.

I wonder if you dream
riots or red soil,
wet stones
or this slow revolution
parching the hearts
of its poor soldiers.

I presume nothing, having
no rights among your dreams.
The umbrella palm whispers
for water, you open the tap.

I watch you step lightly
over the grass, intent,
not smiling but happy,
happy enough.

The garden prevails.
The garden does not fade,
will never go blind,
kills no one,
and conquers
by living.

The Guerilla Soldier

Together, from opposite sides
of the small pagoda, we watched
the wasp attack the fly
and carry it, pierced,
out of the gold shaft
of twilight.

Then we looked at each other.
Mocking eyes, a mouth
wet with bitter water:
his face did not change when I smiled.
The silence became so heavy I knelt.
The Buddha stared past us
as we bowed three times,
wordlessly, almost in unison.

I believe his lips touched
the worn stone. I believe
his lips were made of stone.
Outside, a child began to cry.
His face did not change.

The scent of jasmine
was like fingers
touching my mouth.

Later we sat outside
in the jungle, sharing a cheroot,
remembering the smell
of the tea shops in Mandalay,
the scent of Burma.
Finally I understood the addiction,
the longing for fire,
a chain of fingertips.
To breathe in
means *I am alive.*

Never mind the irony,
it has no meaning here,
many things have no meaning here.
The cheroot is a lantern
the soldier carries in his mouth
as he walks into a tunnel
you and I will never enter.

The red coal burned like a target
among the white fireflies.
The fireflies flickered off, and on,
salting his shoulders, his black hair.
I whispered, They are beautiful.

He turned his head
to look at whatever he could see
of me in the dark.
He said,

> Fireflies make me think
> of their white shirts.

The university boys so often
wore laundered white shirts.

Fourteen of my friends
died, drowned by soldiers
in the lake near the university.
Hundreds more were shot in the road
I walked to school on every day.
Do you understand?

Ni Lay, the girl I would have
married – Ni Lay means sapphire –
was raped, raped again.
She bled to death
from a ruptured uterus.

Yet I am still alive.
My face will never change
because I am a survivor.
I will always be shocked.

I pay for my life each day,
again. No merit is enough.
The fireflies, their white shirts.
Do you understand?

That is why I came to the border.

My life is the memory
of the dead.

The Flood

The war on Burma's borders began over fifty years ago.
It is the longest-running civil war in the world.

In the gold light
of late afternoon
the child lay dying,
his eyes rolled white
with dark veins,
flood of blood-black streams,
as though the mud
beneath the bamboo slats
had claimed him already,
risen up the bamboo poles
and entered him, thick,
blind and ravenous.

The medic was roused
from hounded sleep
while the chickens
scratched beneath
the floor. The medic
had no words, only rapid
necessary movement,
his hands signed the language
of survival or extinction.
He pumped wet rice out
of the shrunken stomach
(the tube rasped against
the child's throat
like a tiny shovel
digging deeper).

Then, hair falling over
his eyes, the medic leaned into
the small malarial heart.
He leaned in deep, listening
for the priceless sound,
song of steady rain
pouring through the body.

He pumped the birdbox chest.
He pumped the soft world
between the ribs, curved bones
slick with sweat like the ribs
of a skiff on the reef.
Then he sat back on
on his bare heels
like a man finished
with praying.
The mother began
to scream.

Light poured in
through chinks in the thatch,
over the half-high walls,
sunlight with honey and bees
in it, *sagawa* flowers, yellow
silk on a wedding dawn,
useless fingers stained
with gold, with ink, the sun
drenched even the sewage mud
with a light no one
ever dies in,
never a child.

He was three years old.
His hair was shorn velvet,
the mark of a new son,
new dead soldier
of the Karen people.

Maw Ker Refugee Camp, 1997

the border

the black-haired women
      on the riverbank
        were wailing, mourning
the village over the hills:
      charred ribs of huts
         skeletons of wood
           and daughters
        soot, ash, blackened pots

first the soldiers
    burned the school
      then they hunted
        for the women, the children

far on the other side
      men galloped
        down the hills
great loping strides
    into the river valley

their almost-bare feet
exploded the hidden mines

voices flew
and red bone-splinters

through the air

at the airport
this is the last time
            she will see him
        before he crosses
            the border

the last time
        his hand
on the glass between them
                now invisible
                now suddenly shining
oh, city of peace –

only handprints will remain
after they are gone
laid finger
to finger, on opposite sides
of the glass

now the agents walk her
out of the air-conditioning
into the dragon's lick of heat
        the shocking light
            the border of flowers
            too brilliant to look upon
    she shields her eyes

he said
you must abandon everything
you must leave your life behind

fake passport, fake name
a non-existence, he sweats
going through customs
his face handsome and calm

certain lies
    (I love you)
are necessary for survival
    (but not the way
    you need)

the definition of failure
    grows very complex
    grows grey hair in the black,
    emerges finally
        triumphant
            the injured
            resolute
            heart

    (No. Not failure but long struggle
    perhaps longer than my life
    I take strength from knowing
    you are alive on this earth.
    Live.
    I cannot live for you.)

the meaning of the glass
is clear:
>   she will never touch him again

later, alone, weeping
>   language of women
>   language of the border

>   she cries
>   amidst the green plants
>   the purple orchids
>   the papaya, cut, with so many black seeds spilling out

>   beneath the lizards singing on the walls
>   she crawls down
>   crashes
>   slides
>   into the hole
>   of sleep

deep in the dream
>   a horse she hears
>   but cannot see
>   gallops away

>   his hoofbeats
>   (her heartbeat)
>   pounding

>   exploding (a landmine)
>   through the chest
>   of the earth

Delicacy

Border town of Mae Sot, Thailand

The prostitute in the Crocodile Bar
hates her pink drink
and needs the man who bought it.
That big green ring.

She is eighteen, very drunk,
her turquoise clothes shimmer
like fake water
as she stands up
and starts to yell.

Her accent is so thick,
he barely understands.
He laughs, What the fuck
are you saying?
while the other men watch,
amused, unconcerned, she is just
another girl ripped
out of her country
by the roots,
stripped down,
made up,
scarlet cheeks,
emerald eyelids.

But it's obvious, they say,
she is just a village girl:
her lipstick is crooked.

She has been here
for a while, she is
already worn thin,
rasped out, the way
you scrape a piece
of the mango clean
with your teeth.

She was sweet once,
they all are, at the beginning,
delicacies from abroad.
They think they've come
to work as maids.
Virgins fetch
the highest price.

The Contract

When you became well again
your friends told you
it had been very difficult
to plan your funeral.

Outside in the market they begged
chicken guts *for the dogs*,
meaning themselves,
and you, burning and freezing,
waking in the night with the scream
still electric in your throat.

Within the fever, you must have known it,
felt your friends' frantic concern:
a burial without earth, or a costly cremation,
all those inedible flowers!
Then they would have to send the news, somehow,
across the border to your family.

It was too expensive to die:
you had to live.
But how to walk back
when your body was sliding away?

Death saved you.

Death came down to the market
in the mood for haggling.

In exchange for your life,
he made you chief scribe
for the subjects of his kingdom,
the people of the border.

Years later, you are still a writer.
You have never failed your contract.
The small circle of light
seeps over the papers on your desk.

Sometimes, late at night,
after your friend is arrested,
after the bodies are found,
you remember dying
almost, in the market,
and your breath spins thinner
than a spider's web.

Longing for peace,
you venture forth, almost,
to the other side,
where Death leans against
the wall of your life,
smiling, waiting,
just waiting for you
to put down your pen.

What she carried

I.

You cannot carry this.
No, not that way, alone.
It is wrong to believe
you have the strength.
You do not.
You, too, are only a child.
You cannot carry this.

Yet you can hold it
for a few hours at a time.
For a day.
For two or three days
when you have known kindness.
You wash the crushed face.
The veil of flies rises.
With practice, you learn
to say *human*.

Now you will carry
part of it
forever.

2.

You are able to pronounce
some word you heard once
from your mother,
from one of the mothers
who cook on these fires,
these women who taught you
how to carry stones on your head, uphill,
these women who wash their children
in the dirty stream where you, too,
will gather the parasites
in the open net of your flesh.
They come as readily as the fireflies,
they glow in you secretly.

Later, when you become ill
and stumble half-blind to the hospital
you will consider, correctly,
        how lucky I am, this hospital.
You will think, with an unforgivable
measure of self-pity, I cannot
carry this, I am too weak
for this sickness, perhaps
I will die here.
But you will be forgiven.

Even when you throw open
your hands, crying,
Take this
I can't carry it,
it's covered in blood
I'm afraid
you will be forgiven.
You will rest.
Shh, the nurse will say, shh.

3.

Aye Aye arrives.
Her hair swings with the rhythm
of her long red skirt.
She lived for years in the jungle.
Don't worry, she says.
She laughs.
She is still very thin,
her thinness will never leave her.
She carried a machine gun.
It was too heavy, half her weight.
Now, with slender fingers,
she carries to me
flowers from Naing Aung.

Aye Aye is humming.
The song is her own.
Through the fever
she holds the flowers
and slowly snaps off
every thorn.

The child dead

She finds she is unable to return.
Though her body steps
off the boat, a dolphin
glistening in each eye.
She carries the small weight
of herself down the harbour.
She is a suitcase without a key
and knows the locks will
have to be pounded open.
It will be difficult
and involve axes and weeping.
The great cement slabs she walks on
heave away the hungry blue sea.
Turkey, there.
And deeper, Asia, the continent
of her fragmentary heart.

She does not arrive.
Despite the greetings, laughter
laced with thick coffee,
the honey of song.
Odd, the scorpions are smaller here,
the colour of watered-down cognac.
Her house is alive with mice, unanswered
letters, the white cocoons
of mysterious creatures.
When she walks into her own absence,
the absence does not go away
but remains like a shadow on her neck.

Lying in the freshly-turned field,
turning in the earth,
she feels her skeleton already there,
beneath her bones.

But understands her life
stayed behind, on the border
she could not cross.

The child dead, after all the struggle.

She holds the donkey skull in her hands,
tightly, wondering at the weight of it,
the worn-out bone as evidence.

She sits on the stones in her sweet desert
of thyme and returns to the terrible jungle,
the wet paths and the women who died.

Dying shone in that place
where everything else remained hidden.
Including the soldiers, the jealous mines
just under a flap of the earth's skin.

She gets up off the ground,
brushes the raw dirt from her legs.
Baffled by the new complexity,
her failure with the language.

The legless men do not laugh
the same way as the others.
As if our legs, she thinks,
were actually extensions
of our tongues.

She sits in the dusty road.
She sits on the terrace stones.
The beauty foreign
from every angle.

She waits for words to come
in any dialect.

They forced him to eat pieces
of his own ears, lips, tongue.
Then they killed him.

What is there to say?

Her mouth is a hole ringed with teeth.
Her hands, cutting into the bread,
picking up a shovel,
become more useless.

The Moth

The moth flies into the lamp
repeatedly. To save her
I do not light
the candles on the terrace.
To give her peace
I turn out the light.
Boat lanterns
and a borough of stars
burns across the bay.
The moth lands
on my knuckle.
She is the smallest angel
in this house
where we lived.

The Musician's Life

1. The concert hall

The restaurant tables
are too small,
and plastic.
The toilets, as usual,
unmentionable.
A thin octopus suffocates
in oil beside the ashtray.

How does it happen
like this, like love,
anywhere?

Three men make music
around the tables.
Two *bouzoukia*, one guitar.
Sweat on steel strings.

Blue and white for the crown
of coming summer, old crimson
for the wine. Lamb's blood
for the field with poppies.
Coffee-black for the ass
of the rare squirrel.
Living flesh-colour for the colour
of their faces and hands.

But how to name
the colour of their singing?

II. The musician works and loves

The cigarette-stained hands
milk sheep all winter,
twice a day, four in morning
dark, four in afternoon dusk,
miserable sheep, milking in the rain,
milking in the snow, but they say
the old gods love a shepherd.
Bastards!

The calloused hands break earth
and bread. Winter-thickened,
the dirty fingers make cheese,
cure leather with oak-nut husks,
search out the faces of stone
for building a wall.
The dirty fingers, sometimes filthy,
pinch a hand-rolled cigarette, pinch
her sweet voluptuous fat, the succulent thigh.
The musician does not play for thin women.

She, and music:
two skins he longs to be inside.

Before he touched her,
she said,
    No.
    First wash your hands.

Swearing, he washed them.

    Use soap!

III. The circle

A man turns
in the circle
sung by his own body.
He is a key opening
the lock of night,
the lock of fear.

He finds
the heart of the wood
and frees it
with his fingers,
with his mouth.

Now his own voice
is revealed
by the instrument

by the small child
dancing around
and around
barefoot
in the sand
to the music
of the sea.

Marie on the island

The smallness of her
body against the hills
becomes more bearable
when she reaches the small church
and turns to look at the sea.

As though the chapel were a temple
she bends to take off her sandals.
The latch gives under her hand,
chilled white envelops her.
Her feet leave marks of sweat
on the cold marble.

Blood gushes down
the horses' flanks.
Blood leaps from the side
of the dragon, splashes
on the ground. Marie thinks,
in her most adult voice,
The dragon is the martyr.
Je m'en fou de St. George!

George kills the poor beast
repeatedly, not just one
stab wound but dozens,
icon after icon
of fabulous slaughter.
She touches them,
then looks for blood
on her fingers.

On the opposite wall,
the Virgin looks on, depressed.
Her eyes are trained
on some distant release.
Not heaven. The Virgin
ignores even the child in her lap:
where did he come from?
She suffocates under glass,
plastered with old women's kisses.

Only old women come here now,
and winter shepherds escaping
rain and wind. Last night,
I tried to tell Marie
about the winter
but she said *No*,
insisting on her version
of paradise.

Marie is innocent of this place.
Nineteen, French, she knows
the island as dream, not memory.
She doesn't want the northern gales,
nor the miraculous white fingers
of snow painting the naked hills.

Now she opens the door and steps out
into the hot scent of thyme.
The sky is tossed down blue on the bluer sea.
The air burns, scraped by yellow thorns.
Sheep bells ring on the far side of the hill.
The last lambs will be born now.
Marble dust in the air.

The blue of her dress
is younger than the blues
of the sea and the sky.
The wind batters her straw hat
sere yellow while the hills far
below eat their rockiness and unfold
smooth as female flesh.

We sit in the shade of a twisted oak
near the spine of the wind-beaten ridge.
The rocks are red-brown among the thorns
and the stone fences like hardened blood,
jealous veins of ownership
up and down the rocky hills
in this realm of sheep and wind.

How the people love it,
this vigorous land,
I have watched
their relentless gardens
thrive between chinks of stone.
I have made myself such a garden.

The wide straw hat shades Marie's face.
The pentagram weave falls
as a sunlight tattoo
on her shoulders and thighs.

I whisper *Listen.*
    Marie turns her head.

~

The ghosts of their voices
rush through the gaps
and narrows of stone.

The silhouettes of women walk over
the northern crest of the hills.
They have come to thresh wheat
on the highest stone terrace.
The threshing floor
sparks in the sun
like an altar
scattered with coins.

The women work, their hair
hidden with scarves,
heavy with sweat.
The cool blueness beckons
far below, down the hills,
but they never enter
the water. They never take
off their clothes
to swim in the sea.

Their bodies are sheep,
owned by men and slaughter.
The women work the hills
without choice, chaff
and thorns embedded
in their skirts.
When a thorn pierces a sandal,
they sit down to rest on the stones.

Sometimes their laughter
rings down the valley
like a pagan bell.
Sometimes they whisper
about the other side
of the headland,
what the world becomes
after all the untouchable water.

~

When Marie and I finally reach
the crest of the headland,
the moon washes through our eyelids
like a spectacular white drug.
The path into the valley draws us
down through negative shimmer,
rocks glimmering like turtles
and rabbits out of ebony holes.
Thorn-witch lurks in the rosemary,
whorled faces gather in the olive grove.

A horse whinnies in the metallic dark
and Marie jumps out of her skin,
then back in, laughing,
shrieking at the night.
Walking seaward through fields
of glowing melons, gleaming dirt,
she holds my hand, girl-child
in the alien dark.

We camp above the sea
on the roof of a closed-up
summer house.
The tide returns
what we have thrown away
as bounty.
Waves cast white bones
of donkeys and goats
and women up onto the sand,
then drag them away again,
into the blackness.

　　　　～

Sea-salt wind wakes us.
The water sings us down,
brings us green realm, blue school
of fish and one octopus
unfurling amethyst
in a nook of reef.

Marie flies wet over white sand,
pale dolphin, sea-swallow
holding up the wild sky.

She rises from the water
spilling shine and laughter,
her hair black as the deep belly
of the sea, her flesh
iridescent.

When she walks up onto the hot sand,
she spins like a planet,
water sprays from her skin
like a shower of stars in daylight,
she shines, she dances.

Even the hammer-strokes of sun
cannot pound her newborn shadow
to the burning earth.

The Regime in Athens

Longing is grey
ghosted blue, like the skin
around the eyes of the woman upstairs.
Neither she nor the kid ever look at me.

I know they feel guilty for being crushed,
and maybe they are terrified
of flowers and bread, two things
I am often carrying when we cross
paths in the stairwell. From upstairs
as though from heaven
I hear the roar of the man
but I never hear
the language of those two.
They take it silently,
lying down.

He is killing them
first with his voice,
then with his hands.
Remarkable that I never see
blood, just grey-blue skin.
Often I hear the haunted
cries of the boy.
Thirteen years alive
and already a ghost.

The woman is silent.
Her silence spares us
but he never shuts
the fuck up.
Even when he tries
to teach the kid math
it sounds like
The Evil Regime in Power.

Once, after a long night
of insults and swears,
slaps and crash of furniture,
I called the police.
Then listened to the jovial,
complicitous laughter
of the sergeant, who came
downstairs to tell me
not to waste his time again,
a man's problems
with his family
are private.

Sometimes I long to kill the father,
and in bad dreams, I punch
that lousy cop in the face.

I know it is not the answer,
not the thread
that will lead us out
of this apartment building,
but I wonder if we could take up
some kind of humanitarian collection
to hire an assassin.

But who will do it?
Who will speak
a single word?
Who wants to crack
his legs and arms as he
has cracked her jaw
and his child?

Which one of us will step forward
to push him off the roof
when he goes up there
to stare in frustrated pride
at the Acropolis?

While dancing with the Gypsy boy on Constantina's birthday

I was
brought up
(poison cannot be kept down)
to love a god
who hated me.

Strange, I think of this
for an instant without words,
while dancing with the Gypsy boy
on Constantina's birthday.

The boy makes love to his drum
with hot fingers and palms.
His father smuggles Turkey
back to Greece
inside a clarinet.

Their music is the music of snakes,
coil of pagan in the bones,
snakesong, night-pulsing,
pounding, rising, so purely
human after all.
The smoke opens, falls away
in veils, revealing the men's
ravenous faces, the fire
held in their mouths, the bellies
of wine-filled girls.

The close room whirls
in and out of my body
like a scythe
cutting me down,
then the boy with his drum
sows me again on the bare flagstones
where I spring up full-grown
like sweet corn and sway –

Made for it. Nothing else.
Love is not enough, and even *passion*
fails the boy's joy, his sure knowledge
at the heart of wildness
that only he has the power
to create a woman
so marvellous,
so momentary
she will disappear
when he stops playing –

She dances
as though her body
will take her all the way
home, finally,
farther than that, closer,

to a moment long before God
turned into such a jealous bitch,

a time when he heard the snakes
singing, dancing without legs,
and laughed with great, sad
pleasure in his dark.

Siberia

The old man sits
by the aquamarine oval of water
watching a boy dive again
and again.
The boy jackknifes
into the pool, into life.
His movements are sharp. Are ruthless.
The white splash of candy-blue water,
the scent of coffee on the old man's breath.

The boy knows he is being watched,
he accords himself the old man's
attentive gaze. The old man smiles.
It is sad, this year his hands
have begun to tremble.
Everything is impossible
now, when the body
contains seventy years
and a small measure of wisdom,
now, when the body should win
the finest possible love,
the evenings are dreadful
with salad and Schumann.
The balcony empty but
for the dry stirrings
between his ribs,
as though grasshoppers
were breeding there.

The boy already has a certain way
of smoking a cigarette, he is
versed in his own beauty,
the strong legs, the hair washed
gold by salt and sun, the heavy
treasure of crotch. Water gilds him,
drips from his knees.
His wet footprints follow him longingly,
dripping over the plaques of grey stone.

The brown skin, like his shirts,
will never wrinkle.
Loneliness is the far country,
the cold one, the Siberia
of the failed.
He believes he will never
go there. The climate
would not suit him.

Guidebook

For Philip Marchand

Pray irreverently.
Address the gods
by their first names.
Make inappropriate overtures
to the goddesses.

They will forgive you:
forgiveness is their great labour.
They want you to love them
as though they were human,
that irresistible error.

Do not be afraid
on the maze of paths
in this medieval village.
Do not fear the tombs
at the edge of the market,
ancient graves exposed
and pillaged, a rape
so common the tourists
fail to photograph it.

Be febrile and undisciplined
before it is too late.
It may be too late tomorrow.

Quickly, then, gather yourself
up like earth, like a fistful
of tangled hair,
steel the muscles in your thighs
and back and shoulders –

At the count of three
    push
roll the fallen columns
through the dark
and release the slaves
trapped beneath.

Never tell what you wish for

The stars fall all August,
embarrassing me.
I see so many while others
say, Not one. No luck.

You have to stare at the sky,
I explain, until your neck hurts.
It's easy. It has nothing to do
with luck.

I wish always for happiness
but later crouch bawling
in the field like a wounded sheep.
No, no, nothing is wrong with the stars.
It's just that, occasionally, I tend
to the pathetic.
But then we all do, secretly.
Cry like wounded sheep, I mean.

A sheep is a sweet dumb animal
bereft of certainty.
Yet, when sheep are lambs
it is impossible to believe
they will turn into sheep,
their heads low, their sprightly
fleeced joy gone grey,
matted into the hesitant,
fear-filled duties of the flock.

Maybe I expect too much, as usual.
Of lambs and stars.
Maybe this *is* happiness,
and a wish for what you have positively
creates a negative?
Or maybe the wish itself is the happiness,
that sharp inhalation
when you see the match-head of a star
blown out in the night sky?

Still, maybe *this* is
the wished-for happiness,
after words, very, very late,
walking home alone on the road
above the fields,
past cantankerous goats I love
more than sheep and lambs together,

this is *late* turned into *early*,
the sky laying on fishbone clouds
of rose and mauve, long brushes
of blue roving the air
like a painter who's decided
it's not so bad after all,

the new canvas cannot be black,
the starry night
is beginning to wear thin.

Nightingales

Chill spring evening
on the island.
The sky falls from lilac
to the purple of over-ripe figs
to the dark-blue bruise of Libyan glass.
The sky falls deeply
into the Mediterranean, *medi terre,*
the sea in the rich middle
of the earth, heaven in water.

If we leave the windows open
and play music in the dark,
the nightingales return
to the garden like exiles
coming home.

The Old Woman Speaks

For the women of Psinia

I will point out
the signs to you.
I can do nothing else.

See how you have overlooked
both the bitter yellow flowers
and the blood
though the general beauty
of the landscape made you
reach for your camera?

Am I unclear?
Then follow me
along this beaten road
over these treacherous stones
I love as I love
my own hands.
The same bones, everywhere.

Can you see despite
the unforgiving
brilliance of the light?

Yes, looking away
is less painful,
but it will not
bring you closer.

So far from the hunt,
how can you comprehend
the broken twig
the footprint in the earth
that seems to be twisting back?
You do not notice the threads
snarled on a weed.

And you cannot understand
why I am standing here.

The weed is a plant
the old women know, yellow flowers
in oil to heal, yellow flowers
in tincture to assuage
the pain of birth.

And the white threads?
No, they are not from the hem
of a dress or a veil.
They are the remains
of a wound, a bandage.

Look closely:
there is fresh blood here.

If you do not learn to read
these signs, the traps
will come to you, more dangerous
than wolves.
It is a common fate.

Voiced in the body of a girl
now a woman now turning
to find an aging mother in her face,
in her hands, I am the mother
of a mother.

You see the revolution?
As the moon rises after the sun?
Yet you approach it
as a foreigner, unsure of
where to step on the earth.
You are afraid, surrounded
by their tools of destruction.
I know, daughter, it is true:
they sow the earth
with poisonous seeds.

Yet still there is the child
and the garden
in a secret vale,
still the white goat
and the olive tree,
gnarled as this hand,
hard as these hands
that wake with the dawn
and carve the world
anew, and joyful.

You, too, will learn to tell it.
In pieces, in lengths of cloth,
in clods of earth, broken stones
in your hands.

You will learn to carry
what I carry
because I am old now

I can no longer
go this way
alone, the fruit in my basket,
my grandmother's scythe
the heavy yellow grain

the same bones
are everywhere
daughter

shadow-deep rivers
travel through us

I ask you
to take some of my burden
some of the gift

it is spilling away
I cannot catch it all

help me girl
open your hands

Andreas Amerikanos

On his kitchen table, the ants
march relentlessly toward the bread.
War haunts the island.
You can see it in the way
the old shepherd eats during winter,
bent close over his plate
in the quiet, subdued violence
of hunger. His stomach and mouth still
flood with the memory of emptiness.
Water ran through our veins
the old man tells, never mentioning
the child who shrank to death.

Stronger than the newborn,
his strength enraged him.
How could he outlive
a pure son?

During the summer, this season
of watermelon and music, he does not
speak of the war.
Summer, the myth of paradise
seduces even Andreas.
He wears a sprig of basil
behind his ear.
He chews resin
from the almond tree.

The myth tastes so real
we cannot believe it will perish
like salt on the tongue,
leaving us thirsty
for a truer story.

These fifty years later,
his garden flourishes.
Sometimes at dusk, he stands
in the hand-worked fields,
a weary god in his kingdom,
and he tastes the bitter food
he could not find then.
Sometimes it shrinks his stomach,
this shameless green abundance
at the beginning of his death.

IV

The Border Surrounds Us

I.

Nostos, ancient Greek for sweet.
Algos, the old word for home.
In the original sense, *nostalgia*:
     a pain for the sweetness of home.

     Pain for the sweetness of
          Nowhere, then,
          and Everyplace.

All landscape inhabits us
     but the first is
                    open earth   open sky:
                         prairie
                    the wheat a bonfire of gold
                         around the truck

          my mother
          flying dragon-like
               through twilight
                    cigarette smoke rising
                    from her nostrils

          the cracked grain of her voice:
               If the prairie is this wide
               imagine the world.

Twenty years later, I begin
     to fathom what she meant.

2.

This land is so narrow
so limitless
it has no name but
border.
The people carry what they have
on their backs
dangling in their hands
(thousands of children
tossed broadside
like wasted seed)

They build a city
of bamboo
tarpaulin
broken mirrors
(thousands of children
haul water, run wild, jump
over tent pegs and rope.
A seven-year-old girl carries
two frogs home from the river
to boil. They squirm heroically
in both her hands. The bullet
around her neck catches the last red light
of the sun. The bullet is an amulet
for protection against death
by a bullet).

The refugees from the other side
build a city
of refuge
on the border.

At night they dream
of the earth they fled,
the soil that sweetened
the crops burned by soldiers.

Come the monsoon,
the river floods.
Rain drips into the blankets,
onto sleeping faces.
Rain pools among the tents.
The children are never dry.
The clothes are never dry.
Despite the name of this place
refugee camp
there is no ark, no dove,
and the devastation will last
longer than forty days and forty nights.

The rain batters
the paper on the ground,
soaks it, tramples it, until the word
refuge is like the body
they found in the jungle yesterday.

No one knew her name,
or her tribe, or her language.
No one knew her direction
of flight. Was she going back
to her ruined fields, or
was she fleeing to the border?

The rain was the last ritual
washing of her body.
No one else would
touch her that way.

Rain and rain and rain
and mosquitoes.
The border between malaria
and sorrow opens wide,
there is much crossing over.
The border manifests itself as fever,
the body's attempt to burn out
a parasite it cannot bear to contain
but must.

Frog-catching amulet-wearing
girl:

the disease
on the border is in us

the war at the edge
of nowhere
is ours

but you are the child
dead
in fever

3.

Another life,
in the country called
Long-Before:

the Algerian in Paris
sang in the subway station,
    crack-tooth below jaunty black hat,
        breath of black tobacco
            black wine

    Everyone crosses the frontier to get here
        he said,
    but no one leaves it behind.

Then described, in perfect French,
    how the French cops beat him
        stinking Arab
        until the blood ran out of his mouth
        like a fountain, the fountain
            of youth, *I was seventeen years old,*
            he said. *I believed in the goodness of man.*
            Let me show you my scars.

Nights he looked
to a high window in any quarter,
found one burning light
        and walked away singing,
        the loneliness shining on his skin
        like sweat, like holy oil.

Dark well, desert well,
black wine, black eyes:
I lowered myself into you
      like a bucket made of bone.

Paris. City of borders,
a new one in every arrondissement.
An underground village of bones
with an asshole cop
in every cavern
subway. A skeleton-hand
grabbed your wrist.
The rattling teeth
demanded your papers
and your name.

Shaquil.
Shaquil.
Shaquil.
You owned your name
and nothing else.

City of frayed clothes. A coat worn
five winters long. City of holes.
The Algerian found threads to lead him on.
I am free, he said, often.
In Algeria, they shot my father.
For Allah. The fuckers.
I will never go back there.
And the French, if they had guns
and a good excuse . . .
The only reason I am free
is because I have no country.

Liberty in Paris.
Claim me, I begged him.
Teach me how to say *heaven*
in your language.
Show me the other
constellations.
Get me out
of this darkness.

Alcoholic, angry, brilliant,
beautifully wrecked,
twice brandisher
of loaded pistol
above my head,
how could I not love him?
He prayed five times a day.
And painted poems
in Arabic calligraphy
on his apartment walls.

What does this one say?

It says,

> My apprenticeship to the maps
> of the world must not end.
> The frontier is a knife's edge.
> The border is my land.
>
> The blade follows the contours
> of my breastbone, my breath.
> It is held upright, beside my heart,
> with a plaster of blood and earth.

4.

The human darkness
quarries too deep.
This wound is like an eye,
made to open.

Starlight rains
in every country
but you will find it
only by speaking,
digging through words
unyielding as clay.

The border surrounds us
without clarity.
There is no certain way to see,
to cross into the good revolution
from the diseased heart of power.
With blistered feet, you reach the frontline,
a frontier in the forest marked
by invisible mines. Mortars roar
in the farther dark
while the women whisper,
naming the night
their burning village bore children,
the night fire bore their children
running, aflame, pierced with screams.

In a nightmare, you enter
those remains, stir
the ashes still hot, soot-grey
like dirty snow. Among the scorched pots
and charcoal relics, heaps of charred
pigs and one burnt dress snared
beneath a stone, amid those deaths
and that ruin, you find shards

of your face

fragments of a broken mirror.

What you witness
severs you from yourself,
then binds you tighter
to the shattered world.
You are disfigured, pounded,
tempered among ashes.

5.

Near the end
of a desolate journey
you meet the border guard
(whose brother is the torturer)

and you smile, because you must
do something harmless to prove
you are harmless, you must show
you are clean (your teeth
are white and not broken),
you speak the language,
you have been here before,
in fact you are from here,
yes, this is your country.

But the border guard is not
amused, he does not
believe, he is paid
to doubt you.

He asks,
Do you have the documents
to prove you are human?

Your heart begins to pound.
It kicks like an animal
trapped in a burning stable.
Sweat appears on your forehead.

The documents!

You push your hands into your pockets.
They become small, fierce rodents,
burrowing, biting the empty pods
of your trousers, the pockets
of your old leather bag, the black
inside the breast of your jacket,
those pockets have holes!
The smile withers,
your heart punches breastbone
 where are the papers
 where are the papers

Here! They are here!
You blink in astonishment
like one saved from the cell,
the burning cigarette,
you open the documents
with trembling hands.

Look, you say, pointing to your
photograph, this is me.
The border guard squints.
He says, You look like someone else.

You think, *Yes, you idiot,*
but your mouth smiles,
you clasp your sweaty hands
like a child dealing
with a dangerous god.

Eventually, he lets you go.
He allows you to enter
your own country.

6.

In the border station,
you hold your unsteady hands
around a paper cup.
What you drink is bitter,
it does not taste
like its memory.

The walls, too, are strange-
coloured, and the footprints
are smaller. Many people
crowd the station, taking leave,
arriving, eating, selling,
greeting each other
(the clamour is like
a whole village
gossiping out loud)

but no one
comes for you.

You drink the warm liquid.
Maybe it was always bitter.

You watch the people for hours.
Someone will appear.
This is your country.

Out of the machine of people,
multitudes of no one, finally
a human face
turns to your eyes
without fear,
without calculation.

You behold a human hand
raised in greeting.
The gesture is guileless,
the hand so willing to touch
that the rough fingers
become the final testament
against weaponry.
And you remember that all hands
testify this way at birth.

Grace is not endless
but it is very long.
It is longer than death,
it floats on evil
and grace persists like a weed,
like passionate song,
on both sides
of the border.

7.

Slowly, certain borders reveal
themselves as undeniable,
the blurred but authentic lines
between what we are and
what we must become.

The hardest frontiers to cross
are the ones inside our skin.
A border shifts between
his fingers like a rusted coin
of great worth or a bullet
or a photograph of someone
he will not see again.
His hands tremble sometimes
as he sits smoking
above the City of Angels.

He excels at the despair
of the extreme moment,
the extreme moment like a note
of impossible music, ringing on
into the rattle and shatter of the monsoon,
through the dry-season dust in his throat,
ringing on for years, through sinews and tendons,
playing him for all he is worth.

He fights beyond his own endurance
and make jokes about the wounds.
Quiet man, he is exiled
by war, nostalgic
for tea shops,
his aging mother,
a certain kind of papaya
sold in small cubes
on the streets of Rangoon,
a saffron-deep, honey-rich
papaya, a pain
for the sweetness of home.

8.

These days my borders are fences,
barriers of stone and ruined wire,
of thorn and branch four feet deep,
three feet wide, walls which must be
negotiated with cunning and an eye for adders.
On this frontier between solitude
and memory, I meet the princely light
of the fields and bow
as though at a dance.

Solitude herself bows
to no one, not even princes.
Solitude is barefoot.
She is a beggar
with starving elbows,
cigarette-stained fingers
and flesh made of pure longing.
She holds my wrists and neck and waist
and sings in time with
the white drum of the sun.

The beginning of loneliness made me
look over my shoulder again,
again, expecting the one
who was about to arrive
and never did, the one who disappeared
as I lifted my head.
Now I glance up expecting nothing
but a ghost, a green lizard or snake
among the stones, spirits
which flee as I step toward them.